THE TOP 300 Contemporary Christian Songs

Leadsheets for Performance and Personal Enjoyment

Compiled by David McDonald

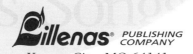
Lillenas PUBLISHING COMPANY
Kansas City, MO 64141

Copyright © 2000 by Lillenas Publishing Company. All rights reserved. Litho in U.S.A

O Magnify the Lord

When Redeemed I Stand

He Holds the Keys

We Will Glorify

Words and Music by
TWILA PARIS

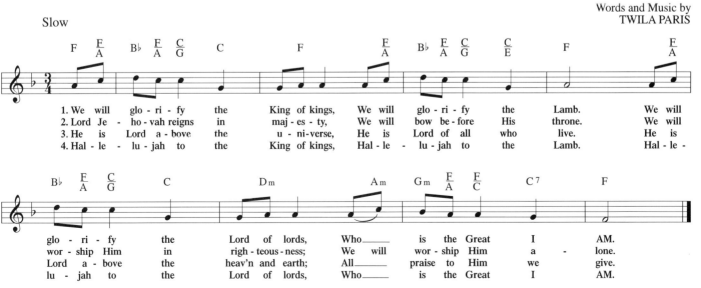

© Copyright 1982 Singspiration Music. Administered by Brentwood-Benson Music Publishing.
All rights reserved. Used by permission.

13

We Bow Down

Words and Music by
TWILA PARIS

© Copyright 1984 Singspiration Music. Administered by Brentwood-Benson Music Publishing.
All rights reserved. Used by permission.

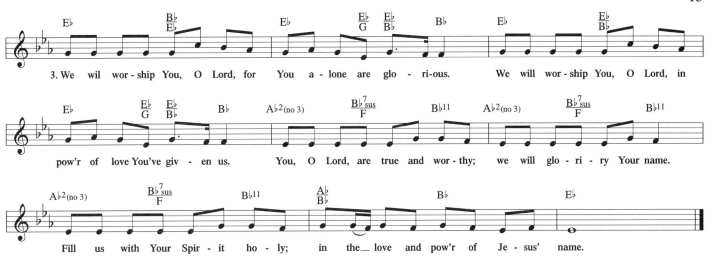

Face to Face

Words and Music by
BUDDY OWENS and BILL BATSTONE

© 1993 Maranatha Praise, Inc. (Administered by The Copyright Company, Nashville, TN).
All rights reserved. International Copyright Secured. Used by Permission.

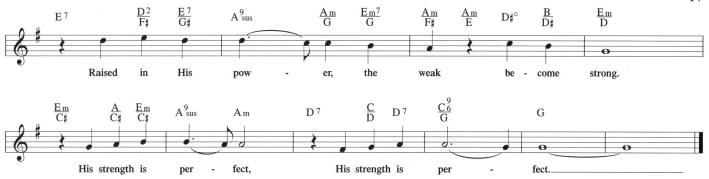

I Can Be Glad

Words and Music by
LARNELLE HARRIS

© Copyright 1990 LifeSong Music Press and First Row Music. Administered by Brentwood-Benson Music Publishing.
All rights reserved. Used by permission.

Grace

Carry the Light

Come Before Him

25

The Battle Belongs to the Lord

Words and Music by
JAMIE OWENS-COLLINS

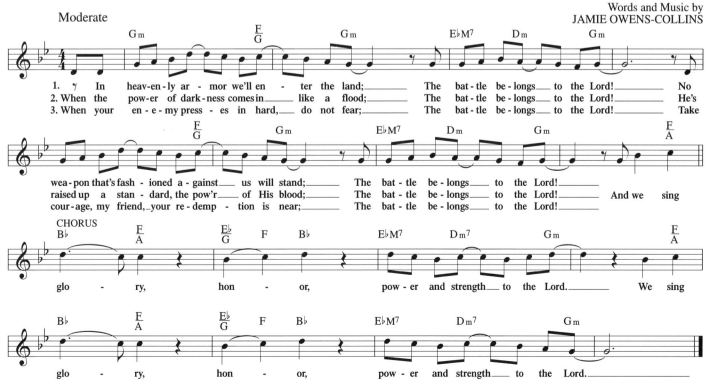

© Copyright 1985 Fairhill Music admin. by EMI Christian Music Publishing. All rights reserved. Used by permission.

Praise You

Words and Music by
ELIZABETH GOODINE

© Copyright 1992 New Spring Publishing. Administered by Brentwood-Benson Music Publishing.
All rights reserved. Used by permission.

God Is in Control

For the Glory of the Lord

Words and Music by
TWILA PARIS

© Copyright 1988 Ariose Music (ASCAP) and Mountain Spring Music (ASCAP). (Admin. by EMI Christian Music Publishing).
All rights reserved. Used by permission.

God and God Alone

Words and Music by
PHILL MCHUGH

© Copyright 1984 River Oaks Music (admin. by EMI Christian Music Publishing). All rights reserved. Used by permission.

Song for the Nations

Words and Music by
CHRIS CHRISTENSEN

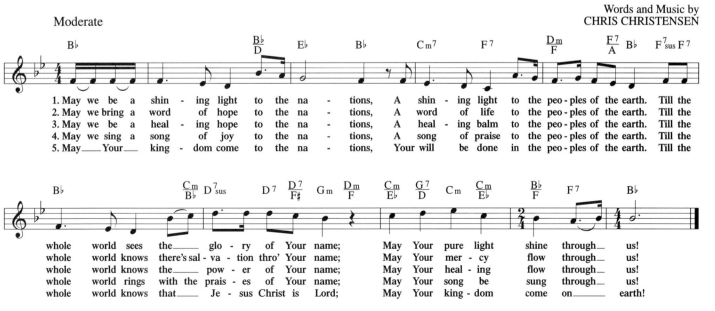

© Copyright 1986 Integrity's Hosanna! Music/ASCAP c/o Integrity Incorporated, 1000 Cody Road, Mobile, AL 36695.
All rights reserved. Int'l copyright secured. Used by permission.

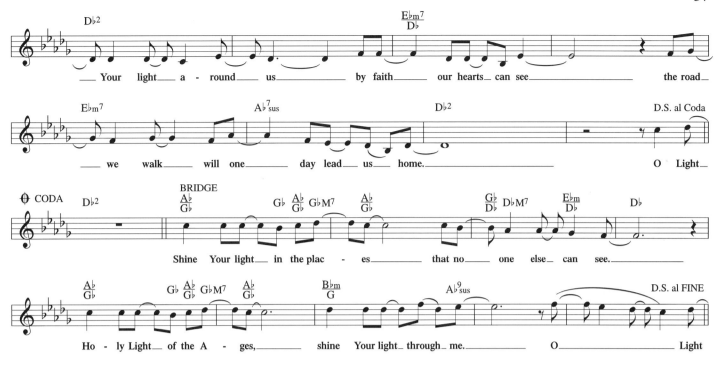

Out of His Great Love

© Copyright 1994 Tylis Music. All rights controlled by Gaither Copyright Management. Used by permission.

Look What God Is Doing

Friends

Words and Music by
MICHAEL W. SMITH and DEBORAH D. SMITH

© Copyright 1982 Meadowgreen Music (admin. by EMI Christian Music Publishing). All rights reserved. Used by permission.

O for a Thousand Tongues

Words and Music by
DAVID BINION

© Copyright 1983 Word Music, Inc. (ASCAP). All rights reserved. Made in the U.S.A. International copyright secured. Used by permission.

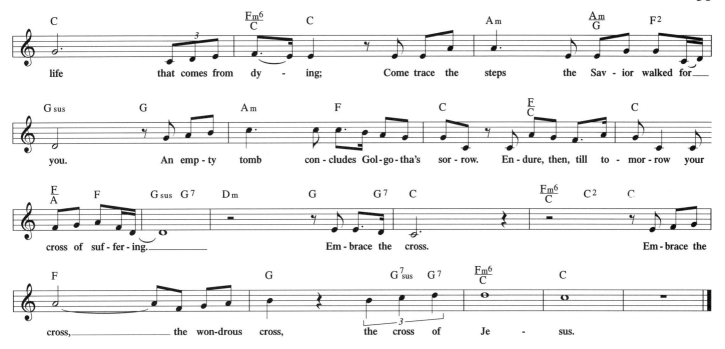

Lamb of Glory

© Copyright 1982 River Oaks Music (BMI) and Shepherd's Fold Music (BMI) (admin. by EMI Christian Music Publishing).
All rights reserved. Used by permission.

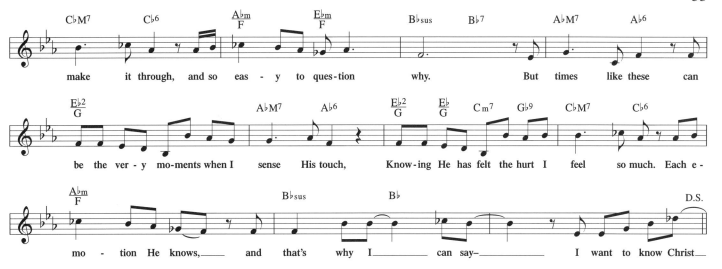

For unto Us

My Turn Now

© Copyright 1988 Singspiration Music (ASCAP) (admin. by Brentwood-Benson Music Publishing), Careers-BMG Music (BMI),
Sparrow Song (BMI) and Greg Nelson Music (BMI) (admin. by EMI Christian Music Publishing).
All rights reserved. Used by permission.

Wounded Soldier

Words and Music by
REBA RAMBO and DONY McGUIRE

© Copyright 1987 New Kingdom Music/RMR. All rights reserved. Used by permission.

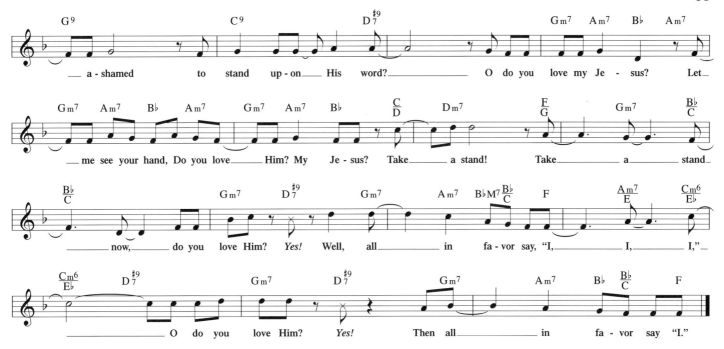

Seekers of Your Heart

Words and Music by
DICK and MELODIE TUNNEY
and BEVERLY DARNELL

© Copyright 1987 BMG Songs, Inc.(ASCAP), and Pamela Kay Music (ASCAP) (admin. by EMI Christian Music Publishing).
All rights reserved. Used by permission.

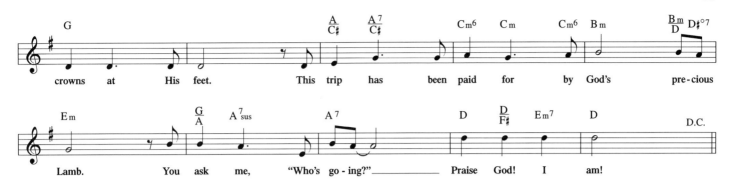

Meekness and Majesty
(This Is Your God)

Words and Music by
GRAHAM KENDRICK

There Is a Redeemer

Words and Music by
MELODY GREEN

© Copyright 1982 Birdwing Music (ASCAP)/BMG Songs, Inc.(ASCAP), Ears to Hear Music (ASCAP).
(All print rights admin. by EMI Christian Music Publishing). All rights reserved. Used by permission.

Let the Walls Fall Down

Words and Music by
BILL BATSTONE, JOHN BARBOUR
and ANNE BARBOUR

© 1993 Maranatha Praise, Inc. (Administered by The Copyright Company, Nashville, TN).
All rights reserved. International Copyright Secured. Used by Permission.

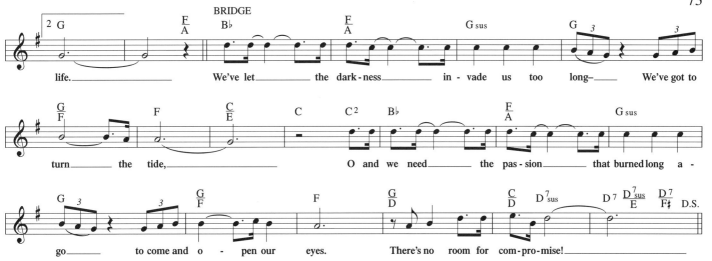

The Reason We Sing

Words and Music by
DICK and MELODIE TUNNEY

© Copyright 1988 BMG Songs, Inc. (ASCAP), Dick and Mel Music (ASCAP) (All rights on behalf of Dick and Mel Music administered by BMG Songs, Inc.), Pamela Kay Music (ASCAP) (admin. by EMI Christian Music Publishing). All rights reserved. Used by permission.

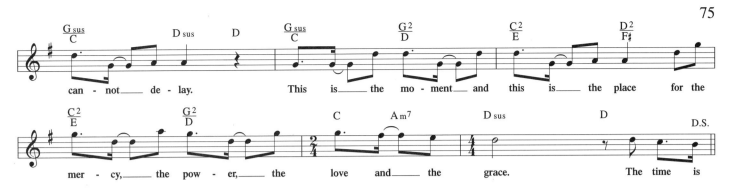

Cherish the Treasure

Words and Music by
JON MOHR

© Copyright 1988 Birdwing Music (admin. by EMI Christian Music Publishing), Jonathan Mark Music (ASCAP).
All rights reserved. Used by permission.

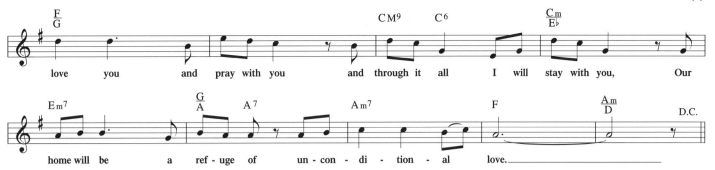

Go Light Your World

Words and Music by
CHRIS RICE

© Copyright 1993 BMG Songs, Inc. (ASCAP). All rights reserved. Used by permission.

Much Too High a Price

Words by PHILL McHUGH
Music by GREG NELSON

© Copyright 1985 Careers-BMG Music Publishing, Inc. (BMI), River Oaks Music (BMI)
and Greg Nelson Music (BMI) (admin. by EMI Christian Music Publishing).
All rights reserved. Used by permission.

My Redeemer Is Faithful and True

Words and Music by
J. I. ELLIOTT and STEVEN CURTIS CHAPMAN

Copyright © 1987 Careers-BMG Music Publishing, Inc. (BMI), Greg Nelson Music (BMI)/
Sparrow Song (BMI)/Birdwing Music (ASCAP) (admin. by EMI Christian Music Publishing).
All rights reserved. Used by permission.

The King of Who I Am

Words and Music by
TANYA GOODMAN and MICHAEL SYKES

Children of the World

Words and Music by
TOMMY SIMS, AMY GRANT
ans WAYNE KIRKPATRICK

© Copyright 1994 Age to Age Music, Inc. (ASCAP) (Administered by The Loving Company/ Careers-BMG Music (BMI)/
Magic Beans Music (BMI)/ BMG Music (ASCAP)/Universal-MCA Music Publishing, (A division of Universal Studios, Inc.)
All rights reserved. Used by permission.

Proclaim the Glory of the Lord

© Copyright 1984 Word Music, Inc. (ASCAP). All rights reserved. Made in the U.S.A. International copyright secured. Used by permission.

Build a Bridge

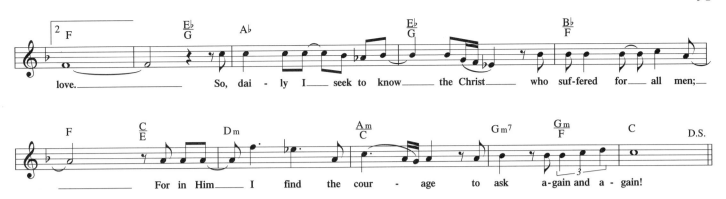

Beyond What I Can See

As the Deer

Words and Music by
MARTIN NYSTROM

© Copyright 1984 Maranatha Praise, Inc. (Administered by The Copyright Company, Nashville, TN).
All rights reserved. International Copyright Secured. Used by Permission.

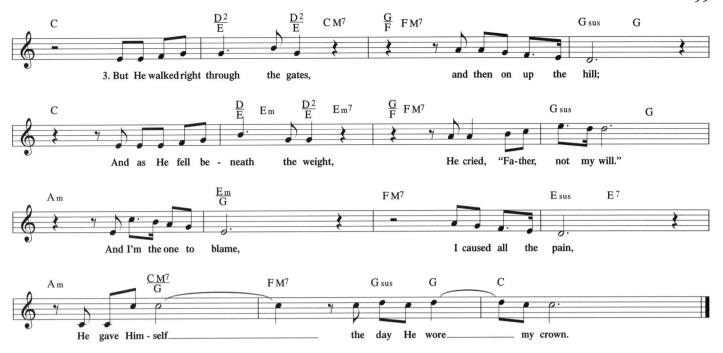

Christ in Us Be Glorified

© 1995 Maranatha Praise, Inc. (Administered by The Copyright Company, Nashville, TN).
All rights reserved. International Copyright Secured. Used by Permission.

Bless God

© Copyright 1988 Lehsem Music, LLC (admin. by Music and Media International, Inc.), Straightway Music (ASCAP) (admin. by EMI Christian Music Publishing). All rights reserved. International copyright secured. Used by permission.

There Is a Savior

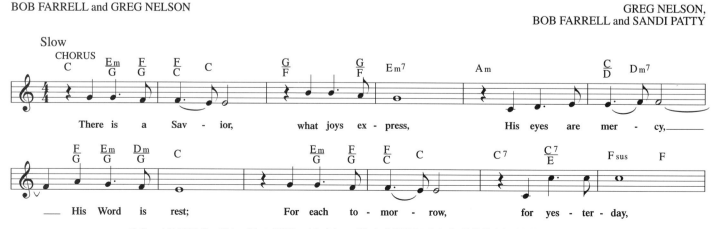

© Copyright 1986 Greg Nelson Music (BMI) and Straightway Music (ASCAP) (admin. by EMI Christian Music Publishing), Careers-BMG Music Publishing (BMI), Summerdawn Music (ASCAP) (Adm. by ICG).
All rights reserved. Used by permission.

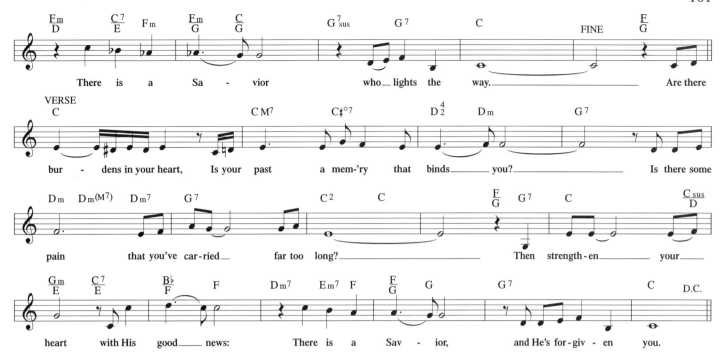

Lord of All

Words and Music by PHILL McHUGH

© Copyright 1987 River Oaks Music (admin. by EMI Christian Music Publishing).
All rights reserved. Used by permission.

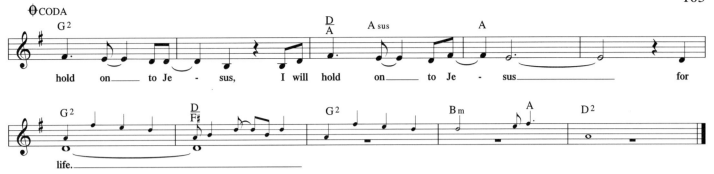

Revive Us, O Lord

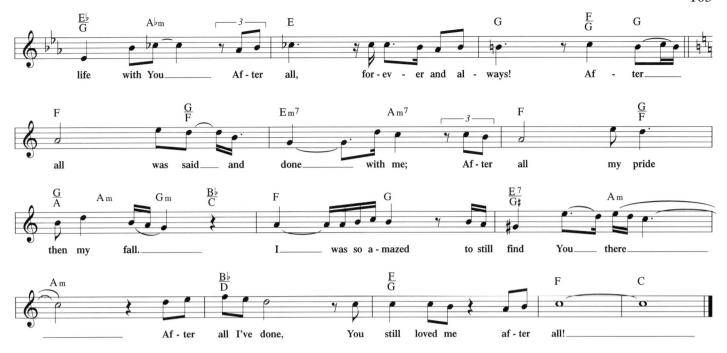

Come Just as You Are

Words and Music by
JOSEPH SABOLICK

© 1994 Maranatha Praise, Inc. (Administered by The Copyright Company, Nashville, TN).
All rights reserved. International Copyright Secured. Used by Permission.

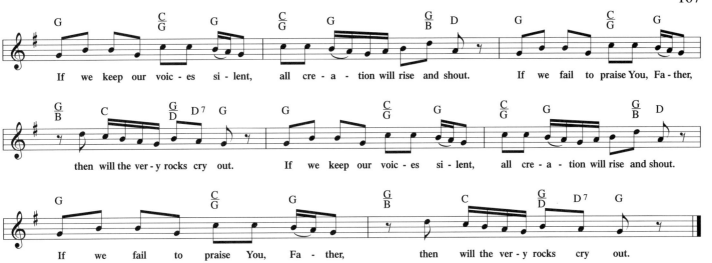

Worthy of Worship

TERRY W. YORK
MARK BLANKENSHIP

© Copyright words 1988 Van Ness Press, Inc. and © Copyright music 1988 McKinney Music, Inc.
All rights reserved. Used by permission.

Magnify Him

Words and Music by
RANDY VADER and KIRK TALLEY

© Copyright 1985 Gaither Music, Kirk Talley Music (BMI) (admin. by ICG).
All rights reserved. Used by permission.

To God Be All Glory

It's Still the Cross

Godly Men

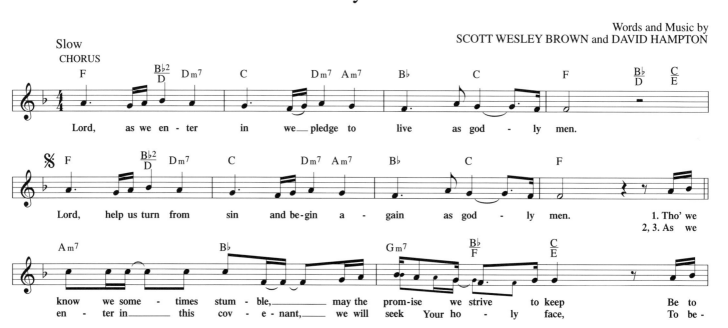

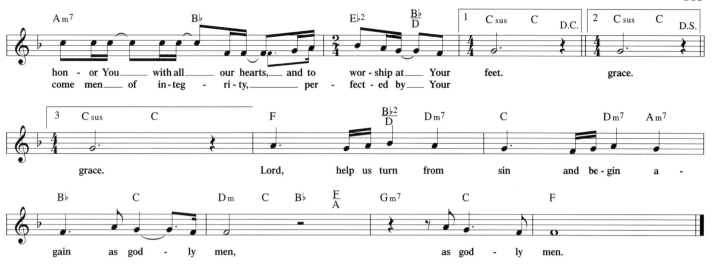

Think About His Love

Slow, in two

Words and Music by
WALT HARRAH

Think a-bout His love,_____ think a-bout His good - ness,_____

Think a-bout His grace that's brought us through._____ For as

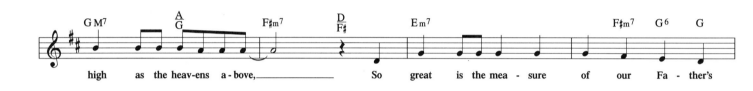
high as the heav-ens a-bove,_____ So great is the mea-sure of our Fa-ther's

love._____ Great is the mea-sure of our Fa-ther's love.

1. How could I_____ for-get_____ His love?_____ How could I_____ for-get
2. E - ven when I've strayed_____ a - way._____ His love had sought me out

_____ His mer-cy?_____ He sat-is-fies,_____ He
_____ and found me. He sat-is-fies, He

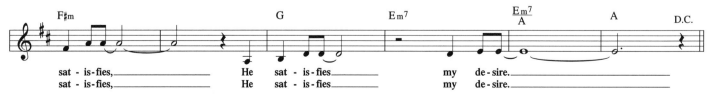
sat-is-fies, He sat-is-fies my de-sire._____
sat-is-fies, He sat-is-fies my de-sire.

© Copyright 1987 Integrity's Hosanna! Music/ASCAP c/o Integrity Incorporated, 1000 Cody Road, Mobile, AL 36695.
All rights reserved. Int'l copyright secured. Used by permission.

117

Lord, I Lift Your Name on High

Words and Music by
RICK FOUNDS

© 1989 Maranatha Praise, Inc. (Administered by The Copyright Company, Nashville, TN).
All rights reserved. International Copyright Secured. Used by Permission.

Love Them While We Can

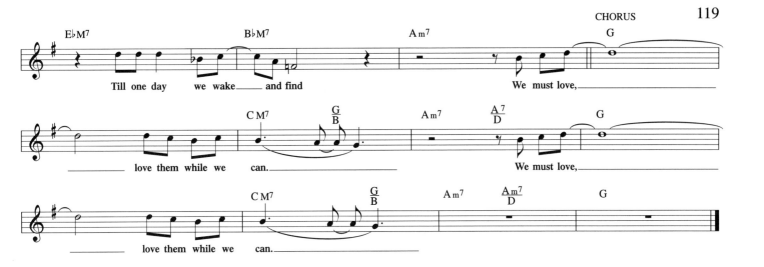

Awesome God

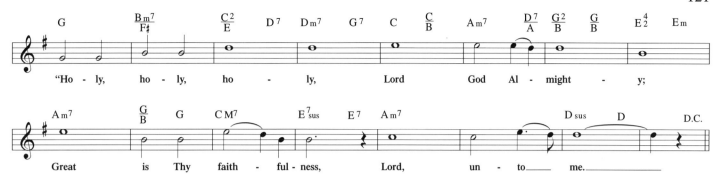

Shine, Jesus, Shine

Words and Music by
GRAHAM KENDRICK

© Copyright 1987 Make Way Music (adm. by Music Services in the Western Hemisphere)
All rights reserved. Used by permission. ASCAP

Wonderful, Merciful Savior

© Copyright 1989 Word Music, Inc. (ASCAP), and Dayspring Music, Inc. (BMI).
All rights reserved. Made in the USA. International copyright secured. Used by permission.

Household of Faith

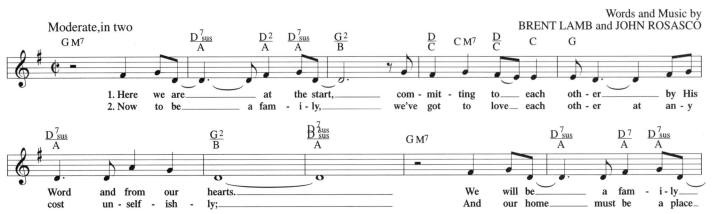

© Copyright 1983 StraightWay Music (admin. by EMI Christian Music Publishing).
All rights reserved. Used by permission.

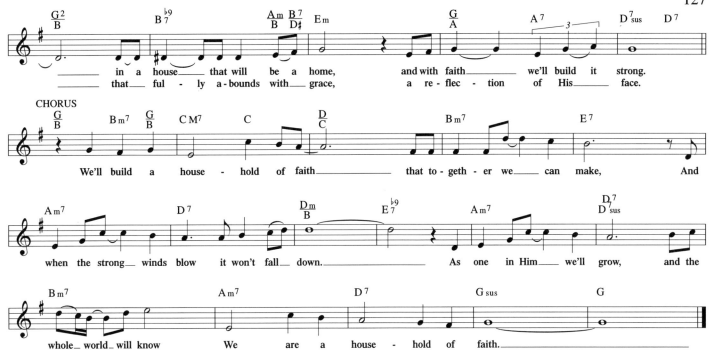

The Joy of the Lord

Words and Music by
TWILA PARIS

© Copyright 1990? Ariose Music and Mountain Spring Music (admin. by EMI Christian Music Publishing).
All rights reserved. Used by permission.

Lamb of God

Words and Music by
TWILA PARIS

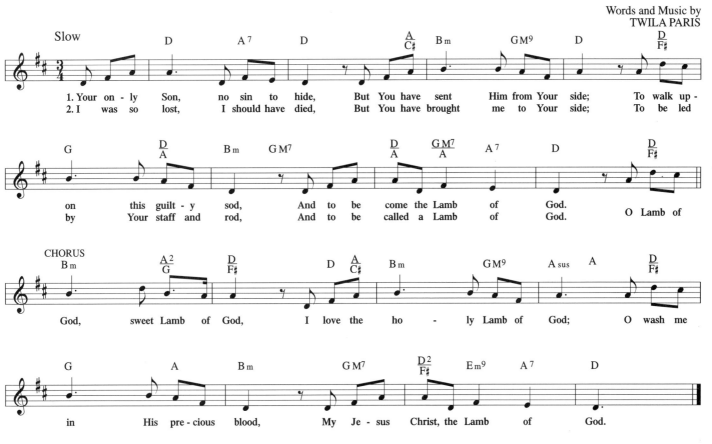

© Copyright 1985 Straightway Music (ASCAP) and Mountain Spring Music (ASCAP)
(admin. by EMI Christian Music Publishing).
All rights reserved. Used by permission.

133

People of God

Words and Music by
WAYNE WATSON

© Copyright 1982 Singspiration Music. Administered by Brentwood-Benson Music Publishing.
All rights reserved. Used by permission.

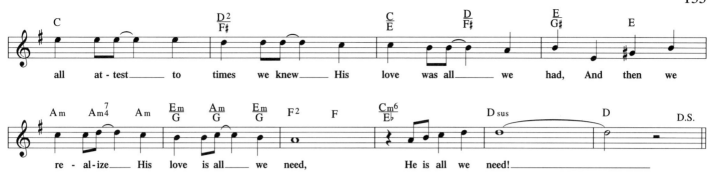

Always There for You

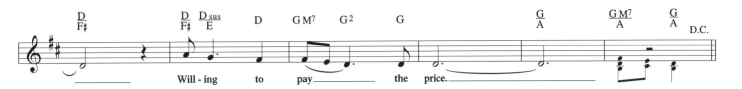

Well Done, My Child

Words and Music by
TONY WOOD and DANNY MYRICK

1. There may be a lonely valley waiting just around the bend.
Many trials will come before I reach my journey's end.
Thro' them I'll be faithful, and I'll walk in victory,
Trusting t'ward the moment when my Father says to me—

2. When I fin-'lly see the streets of gold and the gates of pearl. I
know that I'll forget my every struggle in this world.
Every pain and heartache will quickly fade away.
Trusting t'ward the moment when I hear my Savior say—

CHORUS
"Well done, My child, your race is over. You have fought the fight, you have kept the faith, Enter into the joy of the Lord. Well done, My child, your crown is waiting; Here is your robe of white, your mansion is just in sight, Come into this City of Light, Well done, My child."

© Copyright 1993 BMG Songs, Inc. (ASCAP) and Careers-BMG Music Publishing, Inc. (BMI).
All rights reserved. Used by permission.

I'm Praying for You

We Choose the Fear of the Lord

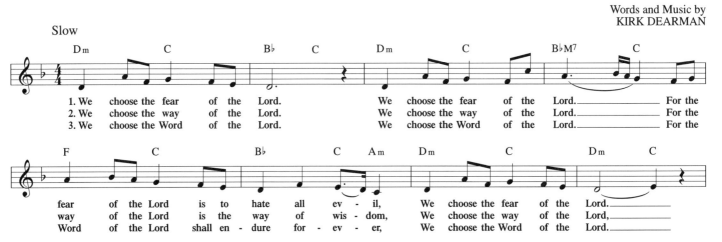

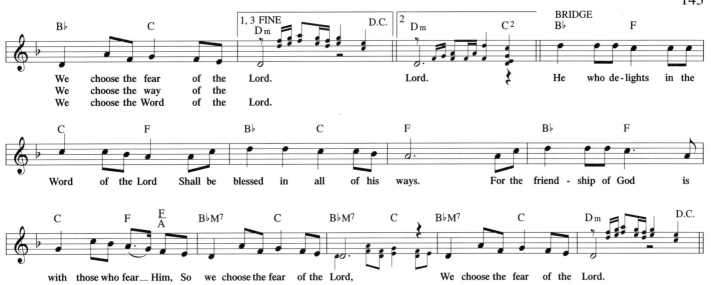

I Call You to Praise

God's Love Never Changes

Words and Music by
DICK and MELODIE TUNNEY

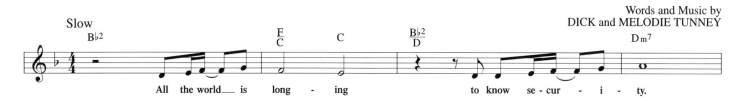
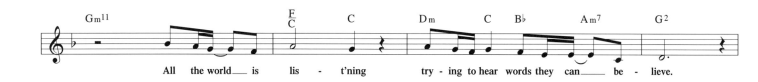
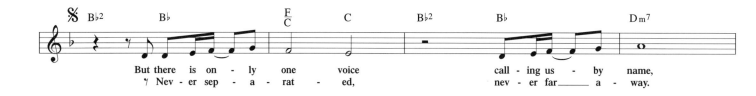
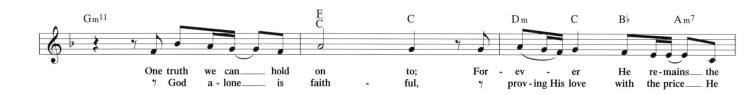

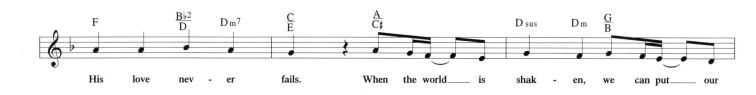
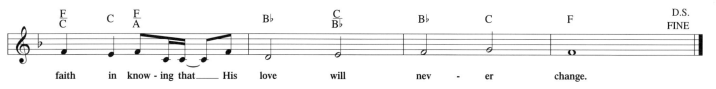

© Copyright 1993 BMG Songs, Inc. (ASCAP), Dick and Mel Music (ASCAP)
(All rights on behalf of Dick and Mel Music administered by BMG Songs, Inc./ASCAP),
and Pamela Kay Music (ASCAP) (administered by EMI Christian Music Publishing).
All rights reserved. Used by permission.

We Are Still the Church

There's Still Power in the Blood

Words and Music by
KIRK TALLEY

© Copyright 1986 Kirk Talley Music (BMI) (admin. by ICG). All rights reserved. Used by permission.

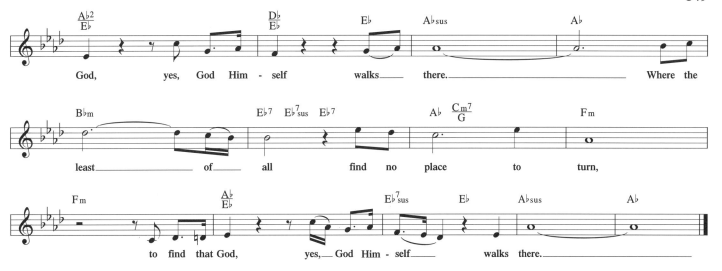

Hallelujah, Praise the Lamb

Words and Music by
DAWN THOMAS, GARY McSPADDEN
and PAM THUM

© Copyright 1984 BMG Songs, Inc. (ASCAP), Magnolia Hill Music, LLC (ASCAP)
(a div. of Smith Music) and Singspiration Music (ASCAP) (both admin. by ICG).
All rights reserved. Used by permission.

In the Presence of Jehovah

Yet I Will Praise Him

GLORIA GAITHER

WILLIAM J. GAITHER
and BILLY SMILEY

© Copyright 1983 Gaither Music Co. and Paragon Music. All rights reserved. Used by permission.

I Will Be Here

Words and Music by
STEVEN CURTIS CHAPMAN

© Copyright 1990 Careers-BMG Music Publishing (BMI), Sparrow Song (BMI)
and Greg Nelson Music (BMI)(admin. by EMI Christian Music Publishing).
All rights reserved. Used by permission.

Holy Ground

© Copyright 1983 Meadowgreen Music Co. (ASCAP) and Songchannel Music Co. (ASCAP)(admin. by EMI Christian Music Publishing).
All rights reserved. Used by permission.

Sound His Praise

© Copyright 1987 BMG Songs, Inc., and Pamela Kay Music (ASCAP) (admin. by EMI Christian Music Publishing).
All rights reserved. Used by permission.

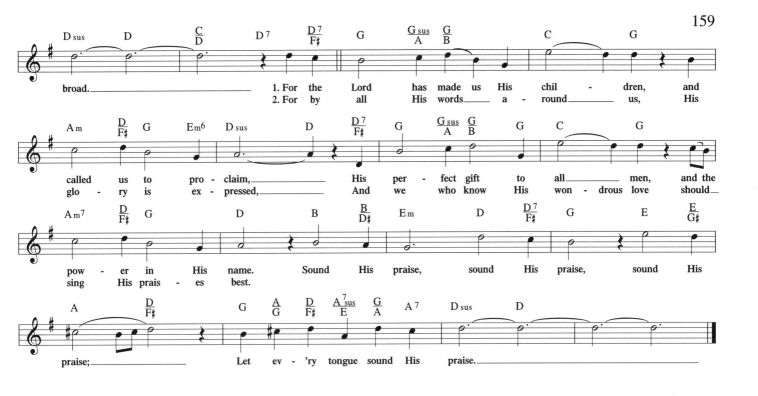

We Are an Offering

Words and Music by
DWIGHT LILES

© Copyright 1987 Word Music, Inc. (ASCAP). All rights reserved. Made in the U.S.A.
International copyright secured. Used by permission.

He Is Here

Words and Music by
KIRK TALLEY

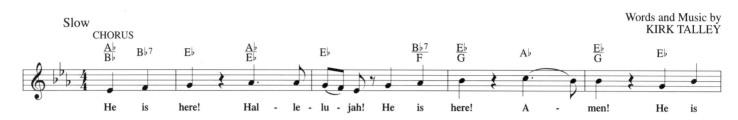
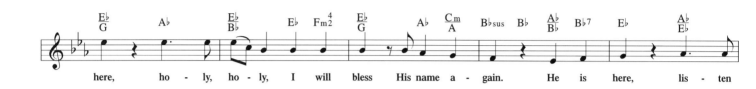

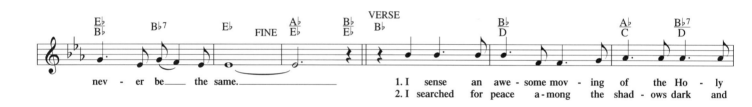

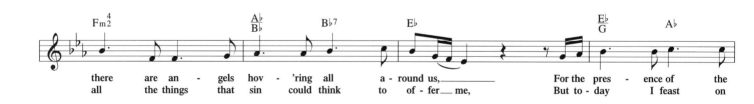
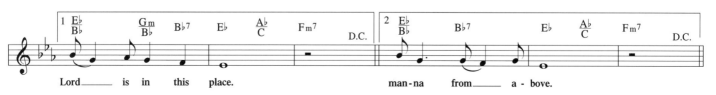

© Copyright 1990 Kirk Talley Music (BMI) (Admin. by ICG).
All rights reserved. Used by permission.

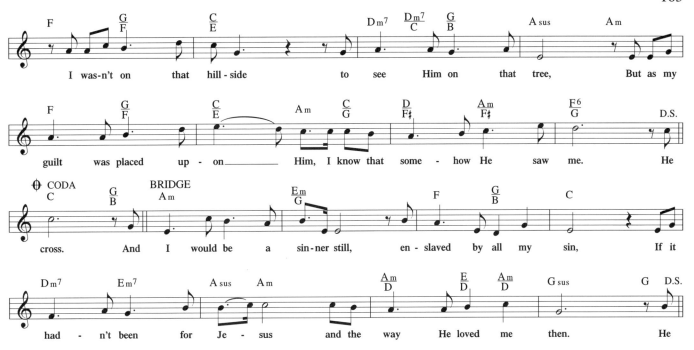

You Are My All in All

High and Lifted Up

Words and Music by
DIANE WILKINSON

© Copyright 1993 Homeward Bound Music (BMI) (admin. by ICG).
All rights reserved. Used by permission.

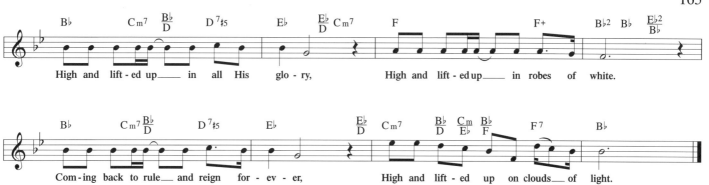

Lead Me, Lord

Words and Music by
WAYNE and ELIZABETH GOODINE

© Copyright 1994 New Spring Publishing. Administered by Brentwood-Benson Music Publishing.
All rights reserved. Used by permission.

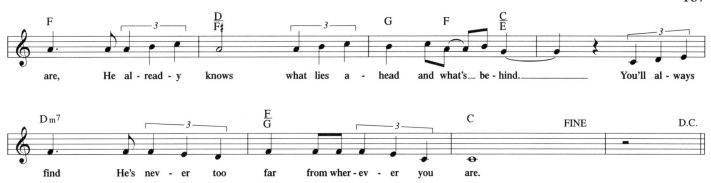

Lord of Glory

You're the Only Jesus

Great Is the Lord

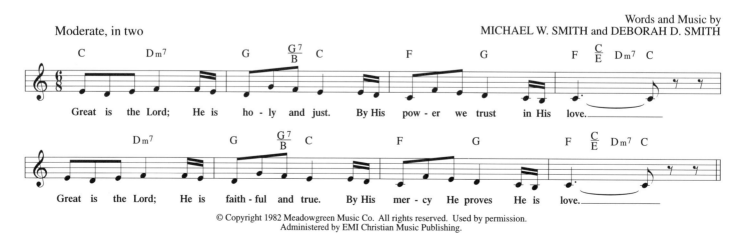

173

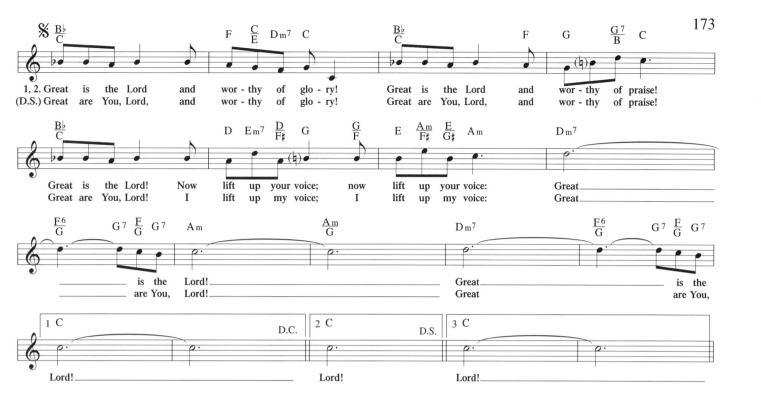

To the Lamb

Words and Music by
SHANNON FOGAL WEXELBERG

© 1993 Christ For The Nations (Administered By MARANATHA! MUSIC c/o The Copyright Company, Nashville, TN)
and Maranatha Praise, Inc. (Administered by The Copyright Company, Nashville, TN).
All rights reserved. International Copyright Secured. Used by Permission.

Antiphonal Praise (We Worship You)

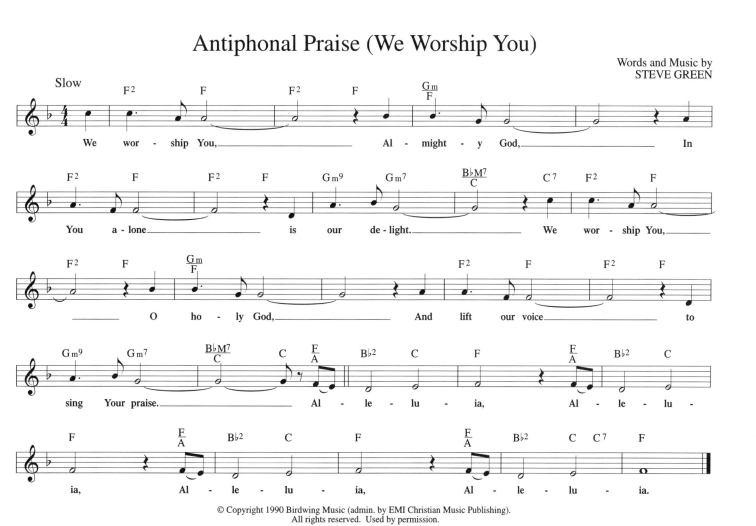

© Copyright 1990 Birdwing Music (admin. by EMI Christian Music Publishing).
All rights reserved. Used by permission.

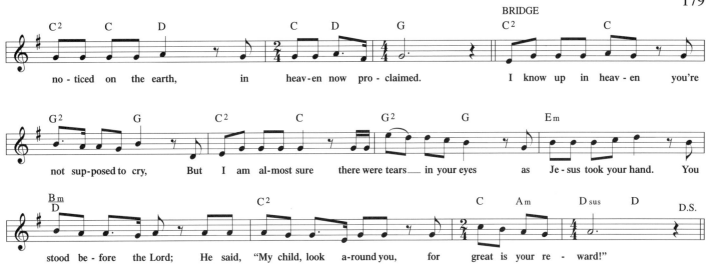

No Other Name but Jesus

Words and Music by
GARY McSPADDEN, BILLY SMILEY
and CHRIS CHRISTIAN

© Copyright 1983 Word Music, Inc. (ASCAP)/ Yellow House Music (ASCAP) and New Springs Publishing, Inc. (ASCAP)
(both admin. by Brentwood-Benson Music Publishing).
All rights reserved. Made in the U.S.A. International copyright secured. Used by permission.

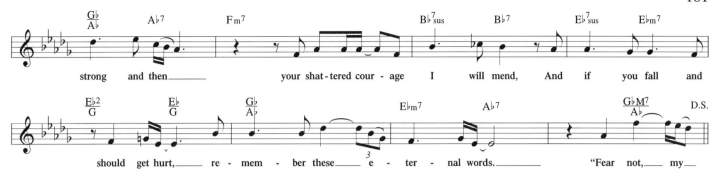

His Word Will Stand

Even the Praise Comes from You

Remember the Lord

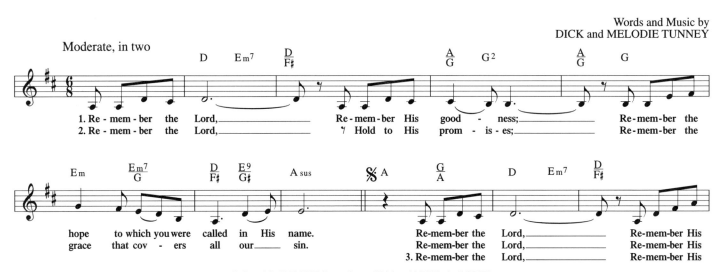

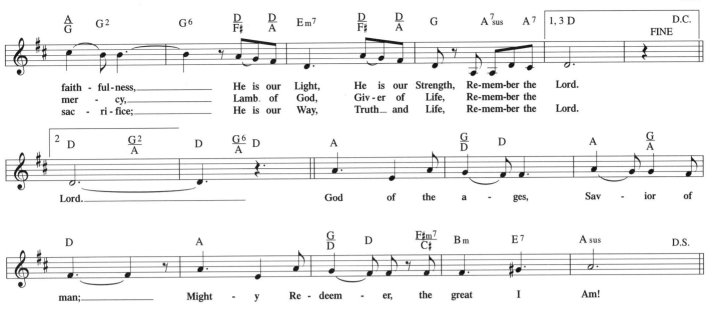

We Are His Hands

Words and Music by
MARK GERSMEHL

© Copyright 1988 Word Music, Inc. (ASCAP). All rights reserved. Made in the U.S.A.
International copyright secured. Used by permission.

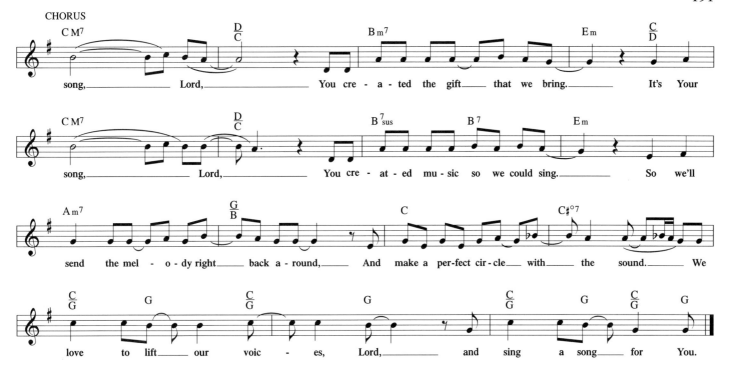

Emmanuel

Words and Music by
MICHAEL W. SMITH

© Copyright 1983 Meadowgreen Music (admin. by EMI Christian Music Publishing).
All rights reserved. Used by permission.

Let Us Praise the Almighty

Favorite Song of All

Heal Our Land

One More Broken Heart

Words and Music by
JEFF SLAUGHTER and DWIGHT LILES

201

Hallowed Be Thy Name

I Will Lift Up My Eyes

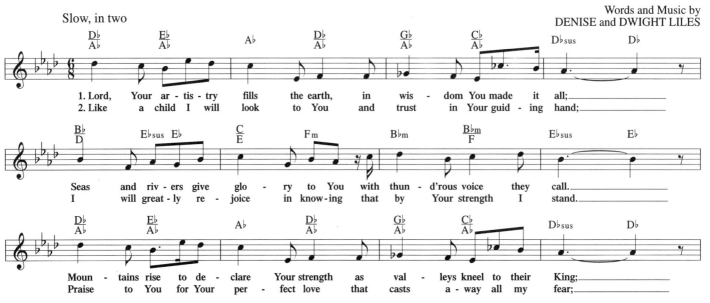

Protector of My Soul

Thanks

Words and Music by
CARROLL McGRUDER

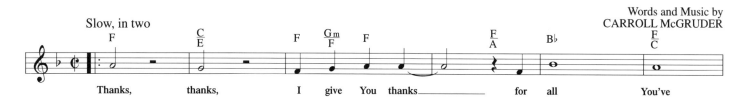
Thanks, thanks, I give You thanks for all You've

done. O I am so blessed; my soul is at rest. O

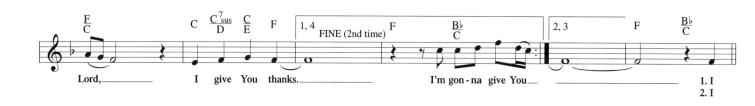
Lord, I give You thanks. I'm gon-na give You 1. I / 2. I

thank You, Lord, for the strength You give to sim-ply car-ry on; Thro' life's
give You thanks this mo-ment, and I will con-tin-ual-ly; For each

toils and tests, in the worst and best, I'm not ev-er left a-lone. You are
day I live, Your grace You give, and I'm blessed a-bun-dant-ly. I

al-ways right be-side me; You hear me ev-ery time I pray; And since I
can't for-get that mo-ment when in my life You made such a change; And since the

first be-gan, You've been my dear-est friend. And I give You all the praise, and prais-ing You I'll say:
Spir-it came, I've not been the same. I just want to give You praise, and prais-ing You I'll say:

© Copyright 1987 Rex Nelon Music (BMI) (admin. by ICG).
All rights reserved. Used by permission.

Beneath His Father's Heaven

Words and Music by
TY LACY and DWIGHT LILES

© Copyright 1993 Ariose Music and Shepherd's Fold Music (admin. by EMI Christian Music Publishing).
All rights reserved. Used by permission.

209

Guard Your Heart

© Copyright 1989 Birdwing Music (administered by EMI Christian Music Publishing).
All rights reserved. International copyright secured. Used by permission.

Revive Us, O Lord

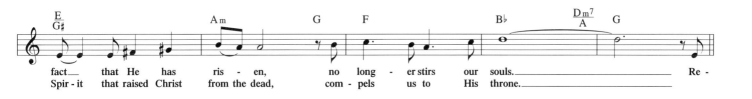

© Copyright 1985 Birdwing Music (ASCAP) (admin. by EMI Christian Music Publishing),
Lehsem Music, LLC. (Administered by Music and Media International, Inc.)
All rights reserved. Used by permission.

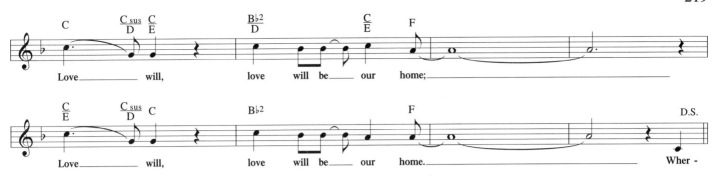

Be Strong and Take Courage

221

O What a Moment

© Copyright 1984 by Beulah Music. Administered by Brentwood-Benson Music Publishing.
All rights reserved. Used by permission.

229

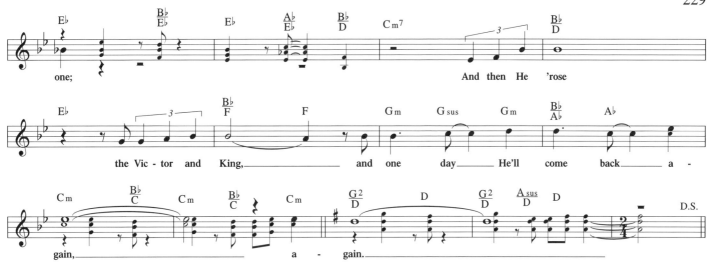

Celebrate the Child

Words and Music by
MICHAEL CARD

© Copyright 1986 Birdwing Music and Mole End Music (ASCAP)(admin. by EMI Christian Music Publishing).
All rights reserved. Used by permission.

Through the Eyes of a Child

Words and Music by
GREG NELSON and BOB FARRELL

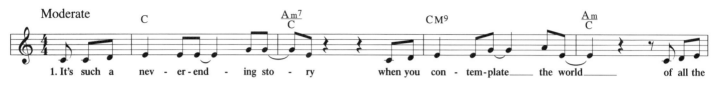
1. It's such a nev-er-end-ing sto-ry when you con-tem-plate the world of all the

ways that serve to hurt our fel-low man. Is the

an-swer, O so sim-ple that we've for-got-ten how to love? When we

wring our hands and seek to un-der-stand, are we

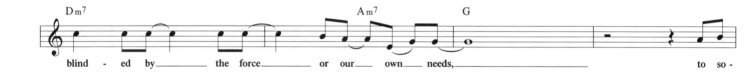
blind-ed by the force or our own needs, to so-

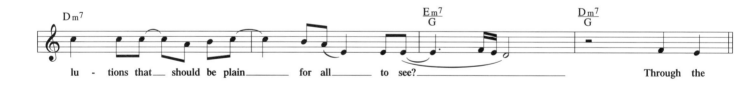
lu-tions that should be plain for all to see? Through the

CHORUS
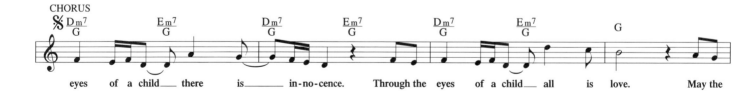
eyes of a child there is in-no-cence. Through the eyes of a child all is love. May the

light of Je-sus help us to see all the world through their eyes. There's com-

© Copyright 1994 Gentle Ben Music (BMI) (Admin. by Dayspring Music, Inc.), Dayspring Music, Inc. (BMI),
Summerdawn Music LLC(ASCAP) (a div. of Smith Music, admin. by ICG),
Lehsem Music, LLC. Admin. by Music and Media International, Inc. All rights reserved. Used by permission.

In Christ Alone

Words and Music by
SHAWN CRAIG and DON KOCH

© Copyright 1990 Paragon Music. Administered by Brentwood-Benson Music Publishing.
All rights reserved. Used by permission.

Only God Knows

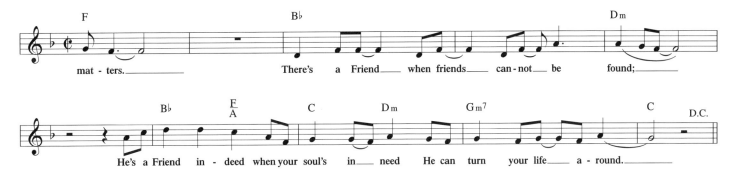

We Are So Blessed

Words and Music by
WILLIAM J. and GLORIA GAITHER
and GREG NELSON

© Copyright 1982 Gaither Music and River Oaks Music (BMI) (admin. by EMI Christian Music Publishing).
All rights reserved. Used by permission.

We Will See Him as He Is

Words and Music by
MARK GERSMEHL and SCOTT DOUGLAS

1. It's as though we see thro' cloud-ed glass, Our eyes can-not see past this veil of tears, our pres-ent pain; This

world can nev-er com-pre-hend a love that will not end, the light that al-ways will re-main. For

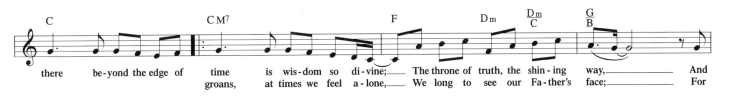
there be-yond the edge of time is wis-dom so di-vine; The throne of truth, the shin-ing way, And
groans, at times we feel a-lone, We long to see our Fa-ther's face; For

soon in maj-es-ty He'll come, He'll take His peo-ple home, and in that bright and glo-rious day We will
there the shad-ows dis-ap-pear; Our eyes will then be clear to see the beau-ty of His face.

CHORUS
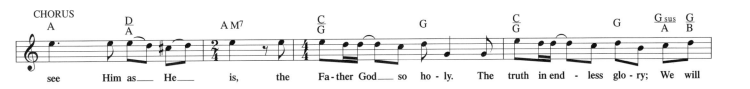
see Him as He is, the Fa-ther God so ho-ly. The truth in end-less glo-ry; We will

see Him as He is. The wis-dom of the a-ges, the love that died to save us, We will

see Him, see Him as He is! 2. Now all cre-a-tion is!

© Copyright 1984 Yellow House Music and Paragon Music. Administered by Brentwood-Benson Music Publishing.
All rights reserved. Used by permission.

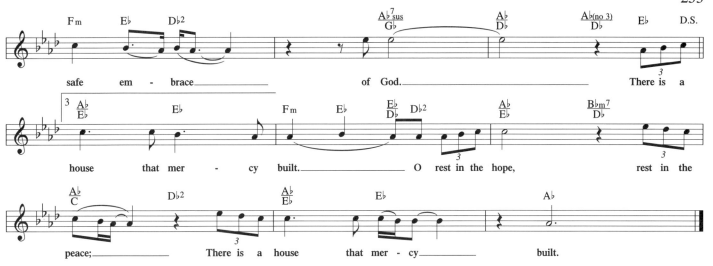

Lion of Judah

Purest Praise

Words and Music by
BILLY SMILEY, BILL GEORGE
and SCOTT WESLEY BROWN

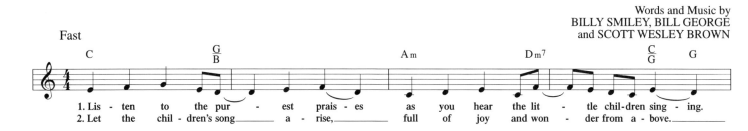

1. Listen to the purest praises as you hear the little children singing.
2. Let the children's song arise, full of joy and wonder from above.

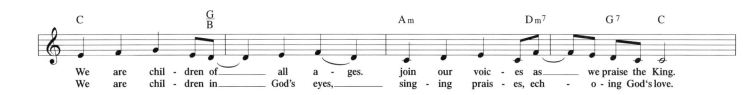

We are children of all ages, join our voices as we praise the King.
We are children in God's eyes, singing praises, echoing God's love.

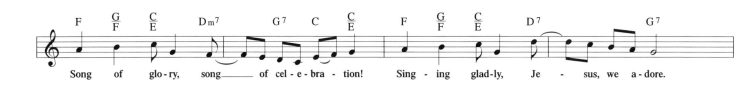

Song of glory, song of celebration! Singing gladly, Jesus, we adore.

Celebrating as a fam'ly, All God's children sing unto the Lord.

CHORUS

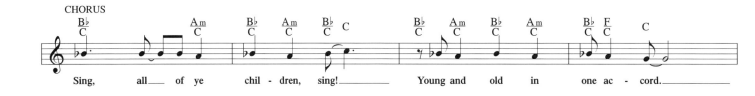

Sing, all of ye children, sing! Young and old in one accord.

Sing, all of ye children, sing a new song before Him. Adore Him!

Let all the nations praise Him, kneeling before the Lord most high.

© Copyright 1984 BMG Songs, Inc. (ASCAP), Pamela Kay Music (admin. by EMI Christian Music Pub.), Yellow House Music (ASCAP) and Paragon Music Corp. (ASCAP) (Both Administered by Brentwood-Benson Music Publishing).
All rights reserved. Used by permission.

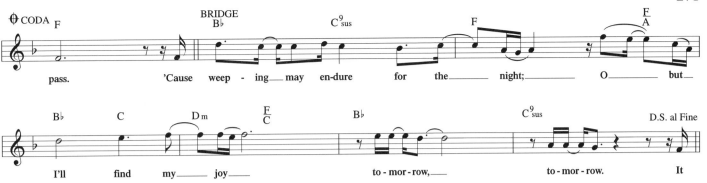

A Time Such as This

Mighty Fortress

JOHN CHISUM and BILL GEORGE
BILL GEORGE

A might-y for-tress is our God, War-rior of the a-

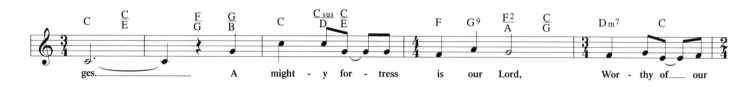
ges. A might-y for-tress is our Lord, Wor-thy of our

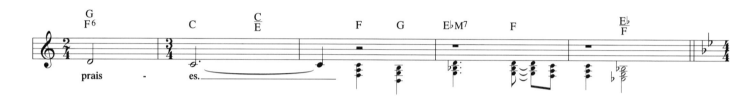
prais - es.

1. Je - sus is the Cap - tain of Sal - va - tion,

Car - ry'ng out His Fa - ther's per - fect bat - tle plan.

Wag - ing war a - gainst the force of dark - ness,

All heav - en's pow'r at His com - mand.

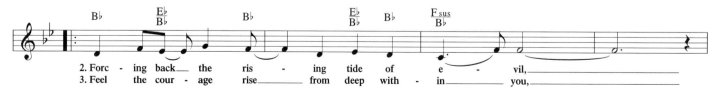
2. Forc - ing back the ris - ing tide of e - vil,
3. Feel the cour - age rise from deep with - in you,

© Copyright 1985 Yellow House Music ASCAP) (Admin. by Brentwood-Benson Music Publishing)
and Ariose Music (ASCAP) (admin. by EMI Christian Music Publishing).
All rights reserved. Used by permission.

Honor the Lord

Words and Music by
GREG DAVIS and GREG FISHER

© Copyright 1985 Paragon Music. Administered by Brentwood-Benson Music Publishing.
All rights reserved. Used by permission.

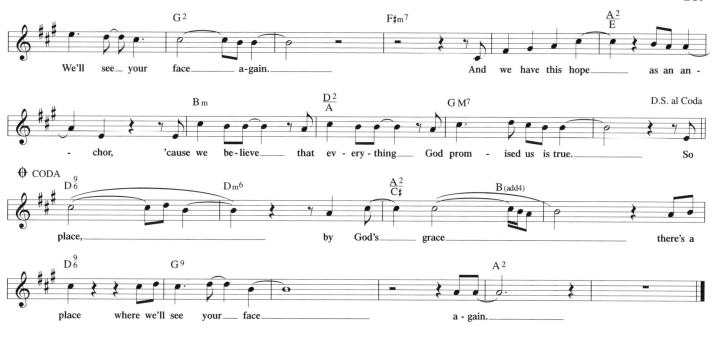

I See the Lord

Words and Music by
CHRIS FALSON

© 1993 Maranatha Praise, Inc. (Administered by The Copyright Company, Nashville, TN).
All rights reserved. International Copyright Secured. Used by Permission.

God Bless the U.S.A.

Words and Music by
LEE GREENWOOD

© Copyright 1984 Songs of Universal, Inc. and Universal-Songs of PolyGram International, Inc. All rights reserved. Used by permission.

305

Yes, Lord Yes

Words and Music by
LYNN KEESECKER

© Copyright 1983 by Manna Music, Inc., 35255 Brooten Road, Pacific City, OR 97135.
All rights reserved. Used by permission.

first I tried to re-sist him, then his hand reached for his sword; And so I knelt and took the cross from the Lord. I placed it on my shoul-der and start-ed down the street; The blood that He'd been shed-ding was run-ning down my cheek. They led us to Gol-go-tha, They drove nails deep in His feet and hands; And yet up-on the cross I heard Him pray, "Fa-ther, for-give them." O nev-er have I seen such love in an-y oth-er eyes; "In-to Thy hands I com-mit My Spir-it," He prayed, and then He died. I stood for what seemed like years, I'd lost all sense of time, Un-til I felt two ti-ny hands hold-ing tight to mine. My chil-dren stood there weep-ing; I heard the old-est say, "Fa-ther, please for-give us, the lamb ran a-way. Dad-dy! Dad-dy! What have we seen here? There's so much that we don't un-der-stand." So, I took them in my arms and we turned and faced the cross, And then I said, "Dear chil-dren, watch the Lamb."

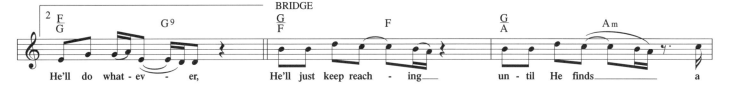

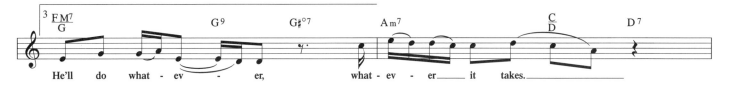

TOPICAL INDEX

ADORATION and PRAISE

All Creation Sings His Praise	154
Arise! Shine!	311
Bless the Lord	211
Christ in Us Be Glorified	99
Christians, Arise	189
Even the Praise Comes from You	186
Exalt the Name	239
Give Him the Glory	291
Great Is the Lord	172
Hallelujah, Praise the Lamb	149
Honor and Praise	43
Honor Him Whom Honor Is Due	273
I Will Lift Up My Eyes	202
It's Your Song, Lord	190
Honor the Lord	279
Joy in the Journey	84
Let There Be Praise	19
Let Us Praise the Almighty	193
Lift Up a Song	129
Lord, I Lift Your Name on High	117
My Tribute	92
O Come, All Ye Faithful	224
O for a Thousand Tongues	49
O Magnify the Lord	3
Praise to the King	14
Praise You	27
Purest Praise	258
Proclaim the Glory of the Lord	87
Sing to the Lord	113
Sing unto Him	248
Sing Your Praise to the Lord	176
Sound His Praise	158
The Joy of the Lord	127
The Lamb Has Overcome	95
Then Will the Very Rocks Cry Out	106
To God Be All Glory	111
We Will Glorify	9
What a Wonderful Lord	287
When Praise Demands a Sacrifice	210
Wonderful, Merciful Savior	126
Worthy, Faithful and Righteous	212
Yet I Will Praise Him	153

ASSURANCE and FAITH

Always There for You	135
Be Strong and Take Courage	219
Beyond What I Can See	91
Dream On	298
Facts Are Facts	302
Fear Not, My Child	180
Find Us Faithful	138
His Strength Is Perfect	16
Hold on to Jesus	102
I Can Be Glad	17
I'll Be Believing	110
Lead Me, Lord	165
Stand Up and Be Strong	33
The Faithfulness of God	134
The Rock of Faith Is Jesus	132
We Choose the Fear of the Lord	142
We Trust in the Name of the Lord Our God	59
With Hope	288

CHRISTMAS and ADVENT

A Strange Way to Save the World	141
Beneath His Father's Heaven	207
Celebrate the Child	229
Emmanuel	191
For unto Us	53
He Left Everything	306
Heaven's Child	188
Immanuel	256
Light of the World	36
Unto Us (Isaiah 9)	255
Worship the King	284

DISCIPLESHIP and GROWTH

Anything That Costs Me Nothing	307
As We Sail to Heaven's Shore	240
Be Strong and Take Courage	219
Face to Face	15
For the Sake of the Call	48
Lead Me, Lord	165
Stand Up and Be Strong	33
We Choose the Fear of the Lord	142
Yes, Lord, Yes	305

EASTER, PALM SUNDAY and RESURRECTION

Easter Song	11
Glorious Morning	196
Hosanna (Smiley)	192
Hosanna (Smith)	299
I've Just Seen Jesus	46
There Is a Redeemer	69

EVANGELISM, MISSIONS and CHRISTIAN SERVICE

Be the One	182
Beyond the Open Door	174
Blessed to Be a Blessing	20
Build a Bridge	89
Daystar (Shine Down on Me)	122
For the Sake of the Call	48
Go Light Your World	77
Heaven in the Real World	82
I Walked Today Where Jesus Walks	148
Look What God Is Doing	39
My Soul Desire	278
Not Too Far from Here	214
One More Broken Heart	200
Outside These Walls	231
Song for the Nations	35
Thank You	178
The Reconciliation Song	197
The Time Is Now	74
We Are His Hands	187
You're the Only Jesus	172

FAMILY, MARRIAGE, BABY DEDICATION, WEDDINGS, and CHILDREN

Another Child to Hold	42
Butterfly Kisses	292
Cherish the Treasure	76
Children Are a Treasure from the Lord	168
Children of the World	86
Guard Your Heart	209
Household of Faith	126
I Want to Be Just like You	34
I Will Be Here	156

Love Them While We Can 118
Love Will Be Our Home 218
The Family Prayer Song (As for Me and My House) 205
Through the Eyes of a Child 232
Turn Your Heart Toward Home 78

GOD'S GRACE and MERCY
God of the Second Chance 222
Grace 18
Grace by Which I Stand 318
His Grace Is Greater 2
Mercy Saw Me 208
That's Where His Mercy Begins 139
The House that Mercy Built 252
We Have Seen God's Glory 265

GOD'S LOVE and CARE
Fingerprints of God 128
God's Love Never Changes 144
He'll Do Whatever It Takes 314
He'll Find a Way 245
In Heaven's Eyes 246
Let Us Praise the Almighty 193
Love Found a Way 184
No Greater Love 244
Only God Knows 242
Out of His Great Love 37
Shepherd Boy 26
Testify to Love 12
That's Where the Joy Comes From 223
The Father Hath Provided Again 123
Think About His Love 114
Wherever You Are 166
Why? 304

GOD'S STRENGTH
Almighty God 68
Awesome God 119
Broken Places 38
Fear Not, My Child 180
God and God Alone 31
God Is in Control 28
Great Expectations 312
He Will Carry You 183
He's Worthy 88
His Faithfulness 295
Mighty Fortress 274
Protector of My Soul 203
The Strength of the Lord 206

GOD'S WORD
His Word Will Stand 181

HEAVEN and SECOND COMING
All Rise 286
I See the Lord 289
In Majesty He Will Come 58
Midnight Cry 56
O What a Moment 221
Shine Down 259
Singing with the Saints 108
That's When I'll Know I'm Home 272
The Lamb Has Overcome 95
Watch and Pray 169
We Will See Him as He Is 251
Well Done, My Child 140
When Redeemed I Stand 4
When the Lamb Becomes the Light 161

HEALING
The River 241
Wounded Soldier 57

JESUS' SUFFERING and DEATH
Broken and Spilled Out 146
Calvary's Love 185
Embrace the Cross 50
He Loved Me with a Cross 162
High and Lifted Up 164
It's Still the Cross 112
Lamb of Glory 51
Lamb of God 131
Lion of Judah 253
Much Too High a Price 79
Remember the Lord 186
The Day He Wore My Crown 98
There Is a Redeemer 69
To the Lamb 173
Watch the Lamb 308
We Will Overcome 262
When Praise Demands a Sacrifice 210

JESUS' NAME
Bless the Name of Jesus 285
Exalt the Name 239
Hallowed Be Thy Name 202
In the Name of the Lord 81
No Other Name but Jesus 179

JESUS (Lordship, Life, Friend)
Bless the Lord 211
Champion of Love 198
Jesus Never Fails 94
Lord of All (Carman) 261
Lord of All (McHugh) 101
Lord of Glory 167
More 247
Shepherd of My Heart 297
Shine, Jesus, Shine 121
Solid as the Rock 155
The Gift Goes On 280
The King of Who I Am 85
The Language of Jesus Is Love 269
There Is a Savior 100
When Answers Aren't Enough 93
You Are My All in All 163
You'll Still Be Lord of All 170

PATRIOTIC
God Bless the U.S.A. 303
Heal Our Land (Brooks) 195
Heal Our Land (Card) 235

PRAYER
Heal Our Land (Brooks) 195
Heal Our Land (Card) 235
I'm Praying for You 142
The Family Prayer Song (As for Me and My House) 205

RENEWAL and REVIVAL
All I Want Is You, Lord 45
All Over the World 277
Bring Back the Glory 66
Come Just as You Are 105
Enter In 75
First Things First 282
Gather at the River 213
Greater Still 260

Hunger for Holiness	300
I Miss My Time with You	238
I Want to Be Where You Are	236
I Want to Know Christ (Driskell)	283
I Want to Know Christ (Tunney)	52
In His Presence	250
It Came to Pass	270
Man After Your Own Heart	199
O I Want to Know You More	290
Revive Us, O Lord (Camp/Carman)	217
Revive Us, O Lord (Mohr)	103
Seekers of Your Heart	61
Teach Me to Love	90
The Basics of Life	72
The Refiner's Fire	216
There Is Peace	70
To Be like Jesus	40
We Are an Offering	159
We Are So Blessed	243

SALVATION, REDEMPTION and FORGIVENESS

After All	104
Build a Bridge	89
Favorite Song of All	194
First Love	130
For God So Loved the World	296
God So Loved the World	220
Hallelujah, Praise the Lamb	149
He Believes in Lost Causes	32
I Stand Here Forgiven	10
I Surrender All	30
Out of His Great Love	37
People Need the Lord	133
The Altar	116
The Invitation	115
There's Still Power in the Blood	147
Prepare Ye the Way	226
That's When the Angels Rejoice	152
The Great Divide	6

SPIRITUAL WARFARE

The Battle Belongs to the Lord	25
The Warrior Is a Child	67
We Will Overcome	262

TESTIMONY and REJOICING

All in Favor	60
All the Glory Belongs to Jesus	268
He Is Able	21
I Am Not Ashamed (Kauflin)	228
I Am Not Ashamed (Thomas)	96
Joy in the Journey	84
Living It Up	175
More than Wonderful	44
My Turn Now	54

No Greater Love	244
Speechless	64
Ten Thousand Joys	234
Testify to Love	12
The Great Adventure	22
Through It All	276
We Are So Blessed	243

THANKSGIVING

Sing unto Him	248
Thank You	178
Thanks	204

THE CHURCH

Face to Face	15
Friends	41
Gather at the River	213
Godly Men	112
House of the Lord	120
How Beautiful	136
Let the Walls Fall Down	71
Love in Any Language	124
People of God	133
Thank You	178
The Gates of Hell Shall Not Prevail	150
The House that Mercy Built	252
The Reason We Sing	73
The Reconciliation Song	197
Triumphantly, the Church Will Rise	62
Undivided	5
Unshakable Kingdom	266
Upon This Rock	7
We Are Still the Church	145
Wounded Soldier	57

WORSHIP AND PRAISE

Antiphonal Praise	177
As the Deer	97
Be Still and Know	55
Because of Who You Are	227
Bless God	100
Come Before Him	24
Come, Thou Almighty King	316
For the Glory of the Lord	29
He Is Here	160
Holy Ground	158
I Call You to Praise	143
In the Presence of Jehovah	151
Lord of All (Carman)	261
Magnify Him	109
Meekness and Majesty (This Is Your God)	63
To the Lamb	173
We Bow Down	13
Worthy of Worship	107

Artist Index

Amerson, Steve
O I Want to Know You More 290

Avalon
Testify to Love 12

Boltz, Ray
Another Child to Hold 42
Lion of Judah 253
Shepherd Boy 26
Thank You 178
The Altar 116
Watch the Lamb 308

Boyce, Kim
Not Too Far from Here 214

Brooklyn Tabernacle Choir/Singers
All I Want Is You, Lord 45
Daystar (Shine Down on Me) 122
Praise You 27
Thanks 204
The Lamb Has Overcome 95
We Will Overcome 262

Brown, Scott Wesley
All Rise 286
He Will Carry You 183
Look What God Is Doing 39
The Language of Jesus Is Love 269

Camp, Steve
Revive Us, O Lord (Camp/Carman) 217

Carbaugha, Damarus
I Am Not Ashamed (Thomas) 96

Card, Michael
Celebrate the Child 229
Heal Our Land (Card) 235
Immanuel 256
Joy in the Journey 84

Carlisle, Bob
Butterfly Kisses 292

Carman
Bless God 100
Bless the Name of Jesus 285
Fear Not, My Child 180
Hunger for Holiness 300
Lord of All (Carman) 261
Revive Us, O Lord (Camp/Carman) 217
The River 241

Cathedrals
Champion of Love 198
High and Lifted Up 164
O What a Moment 221

Chapman, Steve and Annie
Turn Your Heart Toward Home 78

Chapman, Steven Curtis
Be Still and Know 55
Facts Are Facts 302
Fingerprints of God 128
For the Sake of the Call 48
Great Expectations 312
Heaven in the Real World 82
His Strength Is Perfect 16
Hold on to Jesus 102
I Will Be Here 156
My Turn Now 54
Speechless 64
The Great Adventure 22
That's When I'll Know I'm Home 272
The Invitation 115
With Hope 288

Continentals
He Will Carry You 183

Crosse, Clay
I Surrender All 30
Midnight Cry 56

Crouch, Andrae
My Tribute 92
Through It All 276

Crouch, Sandra
He's Worthy 88

Denson, Al
Be the One 182

English, Michael
In Christ Alone 237
Solid as the Rock 155

First Call
Broken Places 38
Seekers of Your Heart 61
Lord of All (McHugh) 101
The Reason We Sing 73
Undivided 5

4 Him
A Strange Way to Save the World 141
The Basics of Life 72
Why? 304

Fry, Steve
O I Want to Know You More 290

Gaither Vocal Band
All the Glory Belongs to Jesus 268
Beyond the Open Door 174
Daystar (Shine Down on Me) 122
Dream On 298
I Walked Today Where Jesus Walks 148
Singing with the Saints 108
That's When the Angels Rejoice 152

Gaithers
We Are So Blessed 243
Yet I Will Praise Him 153

Garrett, Luke
His Word Will Stand 181

Glad
I Am Not Ashamed (Kauflin) 228
In the First Light 254

Gold City
Midnight Cry 56

Goodine Trio
Lead Me, Lord 165

Artist Index

Grant, Amy
- Children of the World 86
- Emmanuel 191
- Sing Your Praise to the Lord 176

Green, Keith
- Grace by Which I Stand 318
- There Is a Redeemer 69

Green, Steve
- Antiphonal Praise (We Worship You) 177
- As We Sail to Heaven's Shore 240
  (duet with Wintley Phipps)
- Bring Back the Glory 66
- Broken and Spilled Out 146
- Calvary's Love 185
- Cherish the Treasure 76
- Children Are a Treasure from the Lord 168
- Embrace the Cross 50
- Enter In 75
- Find Us Faithful 138
- For the Glory of the Lord 29
- God and God Alone 31
- Guard Your Heart 209
- He Holds the Keys 8
- He Who Began a Good Work in You 264
- Honor the Lord 279
- Household of Faith 126
- I Call You to Praise 143
- Lamb of Glory 51
- Let Us Praise the Almighty 193
- Lift Up a Song 129
- People Need the Lord 137
- Praise to the King 14
- Proclaim the Glory of the Lord 87
- Revive Us, O Lord (Mohr) 103
- Seekers of Your Heart 61
  (trio with Sandi Patty and Larnelle Harris)
- Teach Me to Love 90
  (duet with Larnelle Harris)
- That's Where the Joy Comes From 223
- The Refiner's Fire 216
- We Trust in the Name of the Lord Our God . 59
- When Answers Aren't Enough 93
- Wounded Soldier 57

Greenwood, Lee
- God Bless the U.S.A. 303

Harris, Larnelle
- All in Favor 60
- Beyond What I Can See 91
- Come, Thou Almighty King 316
- For unto Us 53
- God of the Second Chance 222
- Greater Still 260
- He Loved Me with a Cross 162
- His Faithfulness 295
- His Grace Is Greater 2
- Honor Him Whom Honor Is Due 273
- I Can Be Glad 17
- I Miss My Time with You 238
- I Want to Know Christ (Driskell) 283
- I've Just Seen Jesus 46
  (duet with Sandi Patty)
- Mighty Fortress 274
- More than Wonderful 44
  (duet with Sandi Patty)
- Much Too High a Price 79
- O Come, All Ye Faithful 224
- Seekers of Your Heart 61
  (trio with Sandi Patty and Steve Green)
- Teach Me to Love 90
  (duet with Steve Green)
- The Father Hath Provided Again 123
- The Strength of the Lord 206
- When Praise Demands a Sacrifice 210

Imperials
- Even the Praise Comes from You 186
- Jesus Never Fails 94
- Love Them While We Can 118
- Sound His Praise 158
- You're the Only Jesus 172

Jernigan, Dennis
- You Are My All in All 163

Krippayne, Scott
- More 247

Lamb, Brent
- Outside These Walls 231

Lanny Wolfe Trio
- For God So Loved the World 296

Martins
- Grace 18
- Heaven's Child 188
- In the Presence of Jehovah 151
- It Came to Pass 270
- Light of the World 36
- Only God Knows 242
- Out of His Great Love 37
- Stand Up and Be Strong 33
- Wherever You Are 166

Mason, Babbie
- After All 104
- All Rise 286
- Bless the Lord 211
- Hallowed Be Thy Name 202

McSpadden, Gary
- Then Will the Very Rocks Cry Out 106

Mullins, Rich
- Awesome God 119

Murray, Jim
- Christians, Arise 189
- Worthy, Faithful and Righteous 212

Nelons
- All Rise 286

Paris, Twila
- Carry the Light 20
- God Is in Control 28
- Honor and Praise 43
- How Beautiful 136
- Lamb of God 131
- The Battle Belongs to the Lord 25
- The Joy of the Lord 127
- The Time Is Now 74
- The Warrior Is a Child 67
- Watch and Pray 169
- We Bow Down 13
- We Will Glorify 9

Paschal, Janet
- I Am Not Ashamed (Thomas) 96

Patty, Sandi
Almighty God	68
Because of Who You Are	227
Come Before Him	24
Exalt the Name	239
Glorious Morning	196
I Will Lift Up My Eyes	202
I've Just Seen Jesus (duet with Larnelle Harris)	46
In Heaven's Eyes	246
In His Presence	250
In Majesty He Will Come	58
In the Name of the Lord	81
It's Your Song, Lord	190
Let There Be Praise	19
Love in Any Language	124
Love Will Be Our Home	218
More than Wonderful (duet with Larnelle Harris)	44
No Other Name but Jesus	179
O Magnify the Lord	3
Seekers of Your Heart (trio with Larnelle Harris and Steve Green)	61
Shine Down	259
Sing to the Lord	113
Sing unto Him	248
The Day He Wore My Crown	98
The Gift Goes On	280
There Is a Savior	100
Through the Eyes of a Child	232
Unshakable Kingdom	266
Unto Us (Isaiah 9)	255
Upon This Rock	7
We Will See Him as He Is	251
What a Wonderful Lord	287
Worship the King	284

Petra
First Love	130

Phillips, Craig and Dean
Favorite Song of All	194
He Believes in Lost Causes	32
He'll Do Whatever It Takes	314
I Want to Be Just like You	34
Living It Up	175

Phipps, Wintley
As We Sail to Heaven's Shore (duet with Steve Green)	240

Point of Grace
Gather at the River	213
I'll Be Believing	110
One More Broken Heart	200
The Great Divide	6
The House that Mercy Built	252

2nd Chapter of Acts
Easter Song	11

Smith, Michael W.
All Is Well	80
Friends	41
Great Is the Lord	172
Hosanna (Smith)	299

Stryper
Always There for You	135

Sykes, Tonya Goodman
The King of Who I Am	85

Talley, Kirk
He Is Here	160
When the Lamb Becomes the Light	161

Talleys
All Over the World	277
Hallelujah, Praise the Lamb	149
Magnify Him	109
The Gates of Hell Shall Not Prevail	150
There's Still Power in the Blood	147
Triumphantly, the Church Will Rise	62
We Are Still the Church	145

Troccoli, Kathy
Go Light Your World	77

Truth
Jesus Never Fails	94
You'll Still Be Lord of All	170

Tunney, Dick and Melodie
All Creation Sings His Praise	154
God So Loved the World	220
God's Love Never Changes	144
I Want to Know Christ (Tunney)	52
I'm Praying for You	142
Remember the Lord	186
There Is Peace	70
To Be like Jesus	40
To God Be All Glory	111

Watson, Wayne
Love Found a Way	184
Man After Your Own Heart	199
People of God	133

Worley, Karla
Prepare Ye the Way	226
The Rock of Faith Is Jesus	132

Praise and Worship Songs (no artists)
As the Deer	97
Be Strong and Take Courage	219
Christ in Us Be Glorified	99
Come Just as You Are	105
Face to Face	15
Godly Men	112
He Is Able	21
Heal Our Land (Brooks)	195
Holy Ground	158
I Look to the Shepherd	206
I See the Lord	289
I Want to Be Where You Are	236
Let the Walls Fall Down	71
Lord, I Lift Your Name on High	117
Meekness and Majesty (This Is Your God)	63
No Greater Love	244
O for a Thousand Tongues	49
Protector of My Soul	203
Shine, Jesus, Shine	121
Song for the Nations	35
Think About His Love	114
The Family Prayer Song (As for Me and My House)	205
The Reconciliation Song	197
To the Lamb	173
We Are an Offering	159
We Are His Hands	187
We Choose the Fear of the Lord	142
Worthy of Worship	107
Yes, Lord, Yes	305

ALPHABETICAL INDEX

A Strange Way to Save the World	141
A Time Such as This	271
After All	104
All Creation Sings His Praise	154
All I Want Is You, Lord	45
All in Favor	60
All Over the World	277
All Rise	286
All the Glory Belongs to Jesus	268
Almighty God	68
Always There for You	135
Another Child to Hold	42
Antiphonal Praise (We Worship You)	177
Anything That Costs Me Nothing	307
Arise! Shine!	311
As the Deer	97
As We Sail to Heaven's Shore	240
Awesome God	119
Be Still and Know	55
Be Strong and Take Courage	219
Be the One	182
Because of Who You Are	227
Beneath His Father's Heaven	207
Beyond the Open Door	174
Beyond What I Can See	91
Bless God	100
Bless the Lord	211
Bless the Name of Jesus	285
Blessed to Be a Blessing	230
Bring Back the Glory	66
Broken and Spilled Out	146
Broken Places	38
Build a Bridge	89
Butterfly Kisses	292
Calvary's Love	185
Carry the Light	20
Celebrate the Child	229
Champion of Love	198
Cherish the Treasure	76
Children Are a Treasure from the Lord	168
Children of the World	86
Christ in Us Be Glorified	99
Christians, Arise	189
Come Before Him	24
Come Just as You Are	105
Come, Thou Almighty King	316
Daystar (Shine Down on Me)	122
Dream On	298
Easter Song	11
Embrace the Cross	50
Emmanuel	191
Enter In	75
Even the Praise Comes from You	186
Exalt the Name	239
Face to Face	15
Facts Are Facts	302
Favorite Song of All	194
Fear Not, My Child	180
Find Us Faithful	138
Fingerprints of God	128
First Love	130
First Things First	282
For God So Loved the World	296
For the Glory of the Lord	29
For the Sake of the Call	48
For unto Us	53
Friends	41
Gather at the River	213
Give Him the Glory	291
Glorious Morning	196
Go Light Your World	77
God and God Alone	31
God Bless the U.S.A.	303
God Is in Control	28
God of the Second Chance	222
God So Loved the World	220
God's Love Never Changes	144
Godly Men	112
Grace	18
Grace by Which I Stand	318
Great Expectations	312
Great Is the Lord	172
Greater Still	260
Guard Your Heart	209
Hallelujah, Praise the Lamb	149
Hallowed Be Thy Name	202
He Believes in Lost Causes	32
He Holds the Keys	8
He Is Able	21
He Is Here	160
He Left Everything	306
He Loved Me with a Cross	162
He Who Began a Good Work in You	264
He Will Carry You	183
He's Worthy	88
He'll Do Whatever It Takes	314
He'll Find a Way	245
Heal Our Land (Brooks)	195
Heal Our Land (Card)	235
Heaven in the Real World	82
Heaven's Child	188

High and Lifted Up	164
His Faithfulness	295
His Grace Is Greater	2
His Strength Is Perfect	16
His Word Will Stand	181
Hold on to Jesus	102
Holy Ground	158
Honor and Praise	43
Honor Him Whom Honor Is Due	273
Honor the Lord	279
Hosanna (Smith)	299
Hosanna (Smiley)	192
House of the Lord	120
Household of Faith	126
How Beautiful	136
Hunger for Holiness	300
I Am Not Ashamed (Kauflin)	228
I Am Not Ashamed (Thomas)	96
I Call You to Praise	143
I Can Be Glad	17
I Look to the Shepherd	206
I Miss My Time with You	238
I See the Lord	289
I Stand Here Forgiven	10
I Surrender All	30
I Walked Today Where Jesus Walks	148
I Want to Be Just like You	34
I Want to Be Where You Are	236
I Want to Know Christ (Driskell)	283
I Want to Know Christ (Tunney)	52
I Will Be Here	156
I Will Lift Up My Eyes	202
I'm Praying for You	142
I've Just Seen Jesus	46
I'll Be Believing	110
Immanuel	256
In Christ Alone	237
In Heaven's Eyes	246
In His Presence	250
In Majesty He Will Come	58
In the First Light	254
In the Name of the Lord	81
In the Presence of Jehovah	151
It Came to Pass	270
It's Still the Cross	112
It's Your Song, Lord	190
Jesus Never Fails	94
Joy in the Journey	84
Lamb of Glory	51
Lamb of God	131
Lead Me, Lord	165
Let the Walls Fall Down	71
Let There Be Praise	19
Let Us Praise the Almighty	193
Lift Up a Song	129
Light of the World	36
Lion of Judah	253
Living It Up	175
Look What God Is Doing	39
Lord, I Lift Your Name on High	117
Lord of All (Carman)	261
Lord of All (McHugh)	101
Lord of Glory	167
Love Found a Way	184
Love in Any Language	124
Love Them While We Can	118
Love Will Be Our Home	218
Magnify Him	109
Man After Your Own Heart	199
Meekness and Majesty (This Is Your God)	63
Mercy Saw Me	208
Midnight Cry	56
Mighty Fortress	274
More	247
More than Wonderful	44
Much Too High a Price	79
My Redeemer Is Faithful and True	80
My Soul Desire	278
My Tribute	92
My Turn Now	54
No Greater Love	244
No Other Name but Jesus	179
Not Too Far from Here	214
O Come, All Ye Faithful	224
O for a Thousand Tongues	49
O I Want to Know You More	290
O Magnify the Lord	3
O What a Moment	221
One More Broken Heart	200
Only God Knows	242
Out of His Great Love	37
Outside These Walls	231
People Need the Lord	137
People of God	133
Praise to the King	14
Praise You	27
Prepare Ye the Way	226
Proclaim the Glory of the Lord	87
Protector of My Soul	203
Purest Praise	258
Remember the Lord	186
Revive Us, O Lord (Camp/Carman)	217
Revive Us, O Lord (Mohr)	103
Seekers of Your Heart	61
Shepherd Boy	26
Shepherd of My Heart	297
Shine Down	259

Alphabetical Index

Shine, Jesus, Shine	121
Sing to the Lord	113
Sing unto Him	248
Sing Your Praise to the Lord	176
Singing with the Saints	108
Solid as the Rock	155
Song for the Nations	35
Sound His Praise	158
Speechless	64
Stand Up and Be Strong	33
Teach Me to Love	90
Ten Thousand Joys	234
Testify to Love	12
Thank You	178
Thanks	204
That's When I'll Know I'm Home	272
That's When the Angels Rejoice	152
That's Where His Mercy Begins	139
That's Where the Joy Comes From	223
The Altar	116
The Basics of Life	72
The Battle Belongs to the Lord	25
The Day He Wore My Crown	98
The Faithfulness of God	134
The Family Prayer Song (As for Me and My House)	205
The Father Hath Provided Again	123
The Gates of Hell Shall Not Prevail	150
The Gift Goes On	280
The Great Adventure	22
The Great Divide	6
The House that Mercy Built	252
The Invitation	115
The Joy of the Lord	127
The King of Who I Am	85
The Lamb Has Overcome	95
The Language of Jesus Is Love	269
The Reason We Sing	73
The Reconciliation Song	197
The Refiner's Fire	216
The River	241
The Rock of Faith Is Jesus	132
The Strength of the Lord	206
The Time Is Now	74
The Warrior Is a Child	67
Then Will the Very Rocks Cry Out	106
There Is a Redeemer	69
There Is a Savior	100
There Is Peace	70
There's Still Power in the Blood	147
Think About His Love	114
Through It All	276
Through the Eyes of a Child	232
To Be like Jesus	40
To God Be All Glory	111
To the Lamb	173
Triumphantly, the Church Will Rise	62
Turn Your Heart Toward Home	78
Undivided	5
Unshakable Kingdom	266
Unto Us (Isaiah 9)	255
Upon This Rock	7
Watch and Pray	169
Watch the Lamb	308
We Are an Offering	159
We Are His Hands	187
We Are So Blessed	243
We Are Still the Church	145
We Bow Down	13
We Choose the Fear of the Lord	142
We Have Seen God's Glory	265
We Trust in the Name of the Lord Our God	59
We Will Glorify	9
We Will Overcome	262
We Will See Him as He Is	251
Well Done, My Child	140
What a Wonderful Lord	287
When Answers Aren't Enough	93
When Praise Demands a Sacrifice	210
When Redeemed I Stand	4
When the Lamb Becomes the Light	161
Wherever You Are	166
Why?	304
With Hope	288
Wonderful, Merciful Savior	126
Worship the King	284
Worthy, Faithful and Righteous	212
Worthy of Worship	107
Wounded Soldier	57
Yes, Lord, Yes	305
Yet I Will Praise Him	153
You Are My All in All	163
You're the Only Jesus	172
You'll Still Be Lord of All	170